T0144771

Magnolia Leaves

Magnolia Leaves
Mary Weston Fordham

MINT EDITIONS

Magnolia Leaves was first published in 1897.

This edition published by Mint Editions 2021.

ISBN 9781513134659

Published by Mint Editions®

MINT
EDITIONS

minteditionbooks.com

Publishing Director: Jennifer Newens
Design & Production: Rachel Lopez Metzger
Project Manager: Micaela Clark
Typesetting: Westchester Publishing Services

TABLE OF CONTENTS

Introductory

I give my cordial endorsement to this little "Book of Poems," because I believe it will do its part to awaken the Muse of Poetry which I am sure slumbers in very many of the Sons and Daughters of the Race of which the Author of this work is a representative.

The Negro's right to be considered worthy of recognition in the field of poetic effort is not now gainsaid as formerly, and each succeeding effort but emphasizes his right to just consideration.

The hope, I have, is, that this volume of "Poems" may fall among the critical and intelligent, who will accord the just meed of praise or of censure, to the end that further effort may be stimulated, no matter what the verdict.

The readers I trust will find as much to praise and admire as I have done.

Booker T. Washington,
Prin. Tuskegee Normal and Industrial Institute. Tuskegee, Ala.December 6th, 1897.

Preface

This little volume is launched on the doubtful sea of literature with the hope that the breezes of public opinion may give an impetus to its voyage. I hope that it will be kindly received as simply the harbinger of what may be expected from the generations to come; and shall consider its mission as being fulfilled if it should be the means of arousing and stimulating some of our youth to higher and greater efforts along this line.

Commending it to an intelligent and impartial criticism,

I am, respectfully,
THE AUTHOR

CREATION

"The heavens declare the glory of God and the firmament showeth his
handy work."

O Earth, adore creative power,
That made and gave to man as dower,
This world of beauty rare,
With hills and vales of verdant green,
With rills and brooks of crystal sheen,
Lovely beyond compare.

O Sun, bright ruler of the day,
When first thy power thou did'st display,
Earth must have shrunk in fear,
When like a meteor burst thy light,
Turning today the long, long night,
With radiance wondrous fair.

Thou Moon, pale sister of the Sun,
When he his daily work has done,
Thou comest forth a queen;
A queen in silvery robe adorned,
With tiara of jewels formed,
Of starry orbs unseen.

Ye twinkling stars of milder light,
Though now ye gleam like sapphires bright,
Across yon azure dome,
The day will dawn, that last dread day,
When from yon heaven you'll fall away,
And man to Judgment come.

Thunder and Lightnings burst and gleam,
Frightful and fierce to us they seem
Rending the darkened sky.
Like giants tread the thunder's peal,
The vivid lightnings swiftly steal,
And men in terror fly.

O filmy clouds, of purest white,
With robes of gossamer cased in white,
Ye floating waters pure,
Sometimes to burst in cooling showers,
Sometimes to deluge wintry hours
With your relentless pour.

Thou beauteous Rainbow bursting forth,
With varied hues encircling earth;
The sign to Noah made.
"I place amid the Clouds my Bow"
To show that I will nevermore
Deluge with angry flood.

Mountains and Hills whose snow capped tops
The vast horizon overlooks,
Pyramids strong and sure;
Nor lightnings fierce nor earthquake shock
Can ever sway, for firm as rock
Ye ever will endure.

Thou Ocean vast, oftimes thy breast,
Is calm and still as if at rest,
Like one in quiet sleep;
But soon in anger thou may'st roar,
And madly toss from shore to shore,
And human harvest reap.

Fountains and Rivulets so clear,
That gush amid the valleys fair,
With soft and mellow ring;
As coming forth from glade and wood
Your babblings whisper "God is good,"
Ye make the vales to sing.

Now when all nature swells the song,
When beast and birds the strain prolong,
Shall man from praise refrain?
Then would the rocks and hills proclaim,

All nature crying out for shame,
They who their Maker's image wear,
Should shout and sing till rent the air
With rhapsodies sublime.

Shipwreck

Night and a starless sky,
Ship on wild billows tost,
With tattered sails and opening seams,
And deck bestrewn with falling beams,
Swift plunging to her doom.

Red lightnings round her flash,
Loud thunders crash and roar,
And the noble vessel mounts the crest
Of the reeking waves, then sinks to rest
Mid carnival of woe.

The Petrel soars aloft,
Wailing her hymn of death,
And the dirge like sounds pierce the blackened sky,
While the crew send forth one anguished cry,
Sinking to lowest depth.

Some ships go out to sea
That never more return,
Souls that from heaven in infancy come,
Tarnished and ruined by sin may become,
Like the Dove to the Ark they never return,
But sink as ship to doom.

THE WASHERWOMAN

With hands all reddened and sore,
With back and shoulders low bent,
She stands all day, and part of the night
Till her strength is well-nigh spent.
With her rub—rub—rub,
And her wash, rinse, shake,
Till the muscles start and the spirit sinks,
And the bones begin to ache.

At morn when the sunbeams scatter
In rays so golden and bright,
She yearns for the hour of even,
She longs for the restful night.
Still she rubs—rubs—rubs,
With the energy born of want,
For the larder's empty and must be filled,—
The fuel's growing scant.

As long as the heart is blithesome,
Will her spirit bear her up,
And kindness and love imparteth a zest
To sweeten hard life's bitter cup.
But to toil—toil—toil,
From the grey of the morn till eve,
Is an ordeal so drear for a human to bear,
Which the rich can hardly conceive.

What part in the world of pleasure?
What holidays are her own?
For the rich reck not of privations and tears,
Saying, "she is to the manor born."
So dry those scalding tears
That furrow so deeply thy cheek,
For rest—rest—rest
Will come at the end of the week.

Yes, even on earth there's a day
When labor and toil must cease,
The world at its birth received the mandate
Of the seventh day of rest.
When the sweet-toned Sabbath bells
Break o'er the balmy air,
Then sing—sing—sing
That the morning stars may hear.

For the frugal table spread,
For the crust and the humble bed,
When He to whom all earth belongs
Had not where to lay His head,
Then toil for thy daily bread,
Let thy heart like thy hands be clean,
And rub—rub—rub
Till thy bones all ache, I ween.

With hands all reddened and sore,
With back and shoulders bent low,
Thou hast for thy comfort that rest, sweet rest,
Will be found on the other shore.
Then they who've washed their souls
Will dip in the crystal tide
Of the fountain clear that was oped to man
From the Saviour's wounded side.

The Snowdrop

How comest thou, O flower so fair,
To bud and bloom while wintry air
Still hovers o'er the land?

How comest from the cold, dark earth?
That fostered thee and gave thee birth,
Studding thy brow with snow

Say, didst thou yearn for sunny bowers?
To gladden with thy pure, pale flowers,
The valley and the hill?

Down in the darkness whence thou came,
Hear'st aught of passion, fashion, fame,
Or even greed for gold?

And when the old earth's bosom heaves,
And scatters man like autumn's leaves,
With its low thundered voice,

Thou sleep'st serene with eyelids closed,
No earthquake shock breaks thy repose,
Till comes the breath of Spring.

THE SAXON LEGEND OF LANGUAGE

The earth was young, the world was fair,
And balmy breezes filled the air,
Nature reposed in solitude,
When God pronounced it "very good."

The snow-capped mountain reared its head,
The deep, dark forests widely spread,
O'er pebbly shores the stream did play
On glad creation's natal day.

But silence reigned, nor beast nor bird
Had from its mate a whisper heard,
E'en man, God's image from above,
Could not, to Eve, tell of his love.

Where the four rivers met there strayed
The man and wife, no whit afraid,
For the arch-fiend expelled from heaven
Had not yet found his way to Eden.

But lo! a light from 'mid the trees,
But hark! a rustling 'mongst the leaves,
Then a fair Angel from above,
Descending, sang his song of love.

Forth sprang the fierce beasts from their lair,
Bright feathered songsters fill the air,
All nature stirred to centre rang
When the celestial song began.

The Lion, monarch of the plain,
First tried to imitate the strain,
And shaking high his mane he roared,
Till beast and bird around him cowered.

The little Linnet tuned her lay,
The Lark, in turn, did welcome day,
And cooing soft, the timid Dove
Did to his mate tell of his love.

Then Eve, the synonym of grace,
Drew nearer to the solemn place,
And heard the words to music set
In tones so sweet, she ne'er forgot.

The anthems from the earth so rare,
Higher and higher filled the air,
Till Seraphs caught the inspiring strain,
And morning stars together sang.

Then laggard Adam sauntered near,
What Eve had heard he too must hear,
But ah! for aye will woman's voice
Make man to sigh or him rejoice.

Only the fishes in the deep
Did not arouse them from their sleep,
So they alas! did never hear
Of the Angel's visit to this sphere.
Nor have they ever said one word
To mate or man, or beast or bird.

THE CHRIST CHILD

On a starry, wintry night,
Frosty and cold was the air,
And the lowly vale where Bethlehem stood,
Looked bleak, and barren and bare.

Her streets deserted and dim,
Lit only by myriads of stars,
That with shimm'ring light illumined the night,—
Among them was fiery Mars.

Adown 'mid the valley so drear
Knelt men, in wonder and fear,
For lo! in the distance a bright star had risen
Wondrously brilliant and clear.

Then an Angel's voice they heard
In heavenly tones it said,
To you I bring "glad tidings of joy,"
"Fear not nor be dismayed."

Go follow that star, 'twill lead
To the Christ-child's lowly bed,
Though Israel's King, He sleeps in an "inn"
Where the cattle oft are fed.

Then over the humble place
Where the Royal Babe was laid,
Did the "Star of the East," blest Bethlehem's star,
Irradiate no more to fade.

O! brightest and best they cried,
Our long promised Israel's King,
Shine out from afar, thou bright morning star,
To thee our offerings we bring.

Bethlehem! blest city of old
Like pilgrims to Mecca we come,
To thy hallowed site, on each Christmas night,
The Christ-child's humble home.

Bells of St. Michael

Come and listen to the chiming
Of St. Michael's merry bells,
When the joyous Christmas morning,
All of Bethlehem's story tells.
When they sweetly chime the anthem
"Glory to be to God on high,"
When the children swell the chorus,
Earth to heaven seems very nigh.

On the gladsome Easter morning,
When the earliest flow'rets bloom,
Snowdrops pure and violets purple
Blend to scatter sweet perfume;
Then your happiest notes are poured forth,
Then your Jubilee is heard,
Pealing out in joyful accents,
Chiming, "God is very good."

From that ancient lofty turret,
O'erlooking land and sea,
Peals of comfort have been wafted,
Sounds of gladness o'er the lea.
Many a storm-tost, weary wanderer
Looked to thee as hope's bright star,
Listened to thy mellow chiming,
Smiling as he crossed the bar.

Ah! old bells, beneath your tolling,
Many a form lies buried low,
'Neath the green-sward of "God's Acre,"
Rest they, all their sorrows o'er.
Softly wave the bending willows,
Sweetly sing the birds their lays,
Whilst thy dear old bells are clanging,
They are singing hymns of praise.

Dear old bells your music thrills me,
Whether rung in joy or woe,
They recall the joyous spring time
Of fond mem'ry's "long ago."
Sweetly chime through all the ages;
As time's cycles swiftly move;
Peal forth loudly, God is gracious;
Whisper softly, He is love.

The Exile's Reverie

'Twas sunset's hour, the glorious day
Had in its beauty passed away;
The sun had bathed in golden dyes
This Southern land of sunny skies;
And crimson clouds, like birds of wing,
Did o'er the earth their radiance fling;
While zephyrs sang amid the trees,
And song-birds warbled to the breeze;
For Spring, just bursting into birth,
Had come once more to gladden earth.

Near Pensacola's margin, lay,
Laved by its never ceasing spray,
The exile, from his native land
The dweller on a foreign strand.
And as he lay kind thoughts of home
Like visions of the past did come;
And mem'ry's mirror pictured clear
The starlight of his boyhood there;
The hopes that clustered round his brow,
The shrine at which he loved to bow.

He mused aloud, Oh! Italy!
Land of the chivalric, the free!
Bruce may of Scotland tune his lyre,
But thee alone, can'st me inspire.
Birthplace of beauty! never more
Shall I behold thy vine-clad shore;
The sward where I in childhood play'd—
The haunts deep in the forest shade—
The place where, mould'ring in decay,
The ashes of a sire lay.

Why did I leave thee? As spring flowers
Return no more through summer hours
When once they blossom, bear and die,

No more will bloom neath sultry sky;
So heart of man when hopes have fled,
And love lies buried with the dead,
No second spring time sends one ray
To cheer his path through life's dark day;
Hope's blossoms like the early dew
Once passed away, naught can renew.

Still I live on, and oft, at eve
My isolated cot I leave;
Thence to this lonely nook I hie
To take a glance at days gone by.
Each blue wave hast'ning to its goal
(Fit type of the immortal soul)
In thrilling accents seems to say
Thou'rt nearing fast life's closing day;
Thou soon wilt reach thy better home,
The home where changes never come.

The Snow Storm

Gentle as a maiden's dream,
Softly as the gliding stream,
Falls the glittering, sparkling snow.
With its wealth of crystal pearls—
Shining, pure-white coronals,
With its robe of silvery sheen,
Decking earth like virgin queen.

As the noiseless flakes descend,
As they downward quickly tend,
Floating waves of downy snow.
Garnered from the upper realms;
Harvested by unknown hands,
Culled from cloudland's brightest bower,
Sent to earth as richest dower.

Symbol pure, and emblem sweet!
Type of purity! 'twere meet
That many swell the strain attuned.
Clad with garb like angels wear—
Robed in heaven's holiest gear—
Pure, white snow, I welcome thee,
Hymning lays of minstrelsy.

Maiden and River

MAIDEN: River, why in ceaseless flow
 Must you ripple to and fro?
 Stop a while.
 Lonely on thy bank I stand,
 On your shining, pebbly strand,
 Canst thou not a moment stay
 Through the long, long summer day?
 Stop a while.

RIVER: Child of earth dost thou not know
 Ne'er can cease my endless flow?
 I must go.
 Onward till I reach my outlet,
 Out beyond the golden sunset,
 Seek not then to stay my flowing,
 Onward still I must be going
 To my goal.

MAIDEN: River, when the storms are raging,
 Wind and rain a warfare waging,
 Do you fear?
 When thy waves with whitened crest,
 Toss around in wild unrest,
 Doth thy bosom shake with fear,
 Trembling, lest thy end is near?
 Say, O! say.

RIVER: Child, my race will ne'er be run
 Not till yonder blazing sun
 Fades away.
 Look t'wards the horizon's crest,
 See the mighty Ocean's breast,
 Now its billowy waves are still,
 He who says it is My will,
 Keepeth me.

MAIDEN: River, should'st thou chance to see,
    On thy journey through the lea,
    Snow white sail?
    Reaching out towards the clouds,
    Quivering with its massive shrouds,
    Touch it gently with thy arms,
    Shield it safe from rude alarms,
    It is mine.

RIVER: Child of earth hast thou not heard?
    That He knows of beast and bird
    Every hair,
    Can He not then bring to thee
    Safe from o'er the murmuring sea.
    Mortal child O! ne'er despair,
    "Ship ahoy!" may greet thy ear,
    Soon, ay soon.

MAIDEN: River, then glide sweetly on,
    Till thy goal is safely won,
    Till at last
    Thou dost hear like thunder roar,
    Breaking from the golden shore,
    Awful words from sacred lore,
    Time for thee shall be no more.
    River, farewell.

Chicago Exposition Ode

Columbia, all hail!
May thy banner ne'er be furled
Till Liberty, with her beauteous rays,
Enlighten all the world.
Columbia, to thee
From every clime we come,
To lay our trophies at thy feet—
Our sunbright, glorious home.

'Twas a lovely autumn morn,
And the leaves were turning red,
And the sturdy oaks and graceful pines
Their branches over-spread;
And the breezes softly swept
The hills and valleys o'er;
And the dew-kissed earth with incense sweet,
Crowned forest, grove and flower.

On a grassy knoll near by
Where the rustling leaves were piled,
Knelt a mighty chief of a mighty tribe,
And his band of warriors wild.
For the rising sun had shown
To the trained eyes of that band,
That vessels three, like white-winged birds,
Were steering straight for land.

Whence comes this stranger fleet?
Whence hails this Pale Face crew?
And the chieftain's brow was wrapped in pain
As his tomahawk he drew.
Then, with quivering voice, he said
Some evil may betide;
From the land of the sky this host has come—
Let's haste to the river side.

And the warriors started forth
Like fawns through the forest trees;
When lo! what a wondrous, solemn sight—
"Pale Faces" on their knees!
Before the Holy Cross,
Each with uncovered brow,
Prayed the mighty God, that His blessings e'er
Might this fair land endow.

And the stalwart braves—awe-struck—,
With heads bowed low on breast
As the veteran sailor proudly cried
San Salvador, the blest!
And this first, grand solemn act
Has been chronicled in heaven;
For, from East to West of this broad, fair land,
Has God's benison been given.

Then hail! bright, sunny land!
Home of the free, the brave!
From the eastern shores to the western plains,
Let thy banner proudly wave.
Nations beyond the seas
Shall worship at thy shrine;
Honor and wealth, and matchless power,
Columbia! be thine.

ATLANTA EXPOSITION ODE

"Cast down your bucket where you are,"
From burning sands or Polar star
From where the iceberg rears its head
Or where the kingly palms outspread;
'Mid blackened fields or golden sheaves,
Or foliage green, or autumn leaves,
Come sounds of warning from afar,
"Cast down your bucket where you are."

What doth it matter if thy years
Have slowly dragged 'mid sighs and tears?
What doth it matter, since thy day
Is brightened now by hope's bright ray.
The morning star will surely rise,
And Ethiop's sons with longing eyes
And outstretched hands will bless the day,
When old things shall have passed away.

Come, comrades, from the East, the West!
Come, bridge the chasm. It is best.
Come, warm hearts of the sunny South,
And clasp hands with the mighty North.
Rise Afric's sons and chant with joy,
Good will to all without alloy;
The night of grief has passed away—
On Orient gleams a brighter day.

Say, ye that wore the blue, how sweet
That thus in sympathy we meet,
Our brothers who the gray did love
And martyrs to their cause did prove.
Say, once for all and once again,
That blood no more shall flow in vain;
Say Peace shall brood o'er this fair land
And hearts, for aye, be joined with hand.

Hail! Watchman, from thy lofty height;
Tell us, O tell us of the night?
Will Bethlehem's Star ere long arise
And point this nation to the skies?
Will pæans ring from land and sea
Fraught with untrammelled liberty
Till Time's appointed course be run,
And Earth's millenium be begun?

"Cast down your bucket," let it be
As water flows both full and free!
Let charity, that twice blest boon
Thy watchword be from night to morn.
Let kindness as the dew distil
To friend and foe, alike, good will;
Till sounds the wondrous battle-call,
For all one flag, one flag for all.

STARS AND STRIPES

Hail Flag of the Union! Hail Flag of the free!
That floateth so proudly o'er land and o'er sea
Thy Stars and thy Stripes, in grandeur doth wave
O'er hearts that are true and hands that are brave.

When first thy bright pennant was lifted on high,
When first 'twas unfolded to patriot's eye;
The ovation that greeted thee, rose through the air
Like incense from altars of hearts true and dear.

Hail Flag of our country, when thrown to the breeze
Thy power is acknowledged, far over the seas.
Thy influence so boundless, that none may deny,
Thy potency reaches all lands, 'neath the sky.

Should war like a dark cloud, encircle our land,
With its threat'ning besom o'ershadow the main.
With head lifted high, thou would'st laugh them to scorn
Who from thy tall flagstaff would try to pull down.

Long, long may thy Stripes and thy Stars proudly wave
O'er hearts that are true and hands that are brave,
And ne'er may thy children, resign to the foe
The Flag that was baptized, in blood long ago.

To the Eagle

Fain would I rival thee
Monarch of birds
Soaring so loftily
Up to the clouds!
Spreading thy pinions
And mounting on air,
Ethereally floating
Divinely and fair.

Where is thy resting place?
Where dost thou dwell?
Is the mountain thy home
Or the stern rock thy cell?
Dost thou live in the desert?
Is the forest thy lair?
O, where is thy resting place?
Eagle, say where?

Always tending upward
May this be my aim;
Ne'er swerving from duty
Or shrinking from pain.
'Tis thus would I rival thee
Monarch of birds,
When soaring loftily
Up to the clouds.

The Crucifixion

Why did the sun his beams conceal
As if unwilling to reveal
That deed of mankind on the day
When Jesus, at the altar, lay
A willing sacrifice.

Earth, too, in terror shook, when He
The Mighty, died on Calvary;
When for our sins He bowed His head,
Gave up the ghost, and quickly sped
To regions of the dead.

And some who had for ages long
Been wrapped in slumber deep and strong
Awoke, and by their converse showed
That death no more dominion had
In that He died.

Why did He die? Ah! blissful thought,
When we near death and hell were brought,
He left His Father's courts above—
O, list to such amazing love—
And died to save.

Why did He die? 'Twas love divine
That caused Him all things to resign
A heavenly choir, celestial home,
Exalted seat, seraphic song,
And all to save.

Blest thought! He reigns victorious now,
To whom all earth will shortly bow,
Let men below and saints above
Wonder at such stupendous love,
As caused their God to die.

URANNE

In a far off hamlet near the sea
Where billows oft, in days of storm, and
Nights of darkness rush reckless to the shore;
Where tall, white cliffs like watchmen keep
A life-long vigil; Oft when the morning
Sunbeams gild their lofty peaks they seem
Like massive crystal vases adorned with
Rays of gold.

Hard-by those snowy cliffs,
Shielded safe from cutting winds and icy
Blasts, stood an humble, unpretending cot,
Its low, thatched roof of matted moss
Glimmered, when the morning sun brightened
Up the valley, and east its rays aslant through
The tiny windows ignorant of glass. Its well-
Scrubbed floor shone like polished wood;
And all around an air of quiet, peace and
Love, prevailed.

Within that cosy nest, there
Dwelt three loving hearts, Nay, four, for on the
Very morn when Christmas bells were
Ringing o'er the land, When children of the rich
And children of the poor alike, were talking
Of the Christ-child, and his day, Unto them a
Child was given, And this lovely babe, blest Christmas
Gift,—was richly prized. E'en now she knew her
Father's voice, and leaped with joy at his return.

But ah! the cry of war, broke o'er the land. Cruel
War, that rends the households and the hearts;
That makes fond bosoms bleed; and waters all
The sod with tears, Salty, agonizing tears, which,
When they dry, leave furrows never healing.—
Sorrows, never ceasing.

The mandate came.—
Marco must go. What! leave the dear ones all
Alone. The gray-halted sire sunning himself
Without the cottage door? The little wife in
Blooming womanhood? The cherub who in
Human form had come to bless his home?
Must he leave his treasures and away to
Distant shores, perchance, lay down to die?
O! the thought was death itself. Yet go he
Must. Each day he'd wander through the glade,
Where every blade and tuft of grass was dear,
So dear. All his life from babe to manhood,
Here was spent. Here he grew, and loved,
And wedded. Here the precious Mother in her
Green old age had yielded to the sharp scythe
Of the Reaper Death. Could he leave her?

The day of Parting came. The sun was high when Marco
Rose. The cheery little table decked with snowy
Cloth was laid. Out from their frugal hoard
Came every dainty Uranne could find.
Naught was too good for him. The dear, the
Faithful! He who had done all in human power
To make her life joyous. Truly, she said, as tears
Lingered in her eyes, "My lines in pleasant places
Have been cast."

Well long they tarried o'er that
Meal. It seemed as though 'twould never end,
And yet they were not eating. At last the babe
Stretched forth its chubby hands and with
Infantile speech, broke up the silent meal.

Marco arose,—
Father, adieu. Take care of these as best thou
Can'st. I know the load is much too great for
Thee. Whose silvery hairs are whitening o'er with age.
Do all thou can'st and leave the rest to "Him
Who notes when e'en the sparrows fall."

And now, Uranne! truest and best, I can
Not give thee anymore my heart, for thou had'st
It all long ago. Thy love to me has been like
Silver lining 'mid the clouds of life.
Has opened up my heart to kindlier feelings
For all who on this earth have naught to cheer,
To solace them in hours like these.

But time doth
Fly. Whether the moments teem with joy or
Flit in sorrow. So Marco said, e're yet I go,
Take this bunch of half-blown buds and place
Upon your breast, near your heart, and wear
Them till I come. Let naught divide 'twixt
Thee and them. 'Mid summer's glow or winter's
Cold, loved one, wear them next thy heart.
Their very name, Forget-Me-Not, will 'mind
Thee of thy lover-husband.

Days, weeks,
Months passed by. No tidings yet had
Come to them, in that lone village by the sea,
Ofttimes the sire would hand-in-hand take
Baby for a walk "by the sad, sea waves"—
Then would the little one pick up shells
And moss, and lisp so sweetly with
Infantile grace, that the aged form would
Straighten up, as if once more the fires of youth
Burned brightly in his veins; and his old
Bereaved heart wound leap for joy.

Alas! when early
Spring had come and the little snowdrops
Gleamed in the valley, little Bright-eyes
Faded and was laid beneath them.
O! then the sun went down in blackness grim,
And the whole world seemed devoid of life;
Not worth living, the old man cried. And
Then he, too, alas! was laid beside the babe.

All through the long,
Long summer lonely Uranne dwelt. Her heart
Low down beneath the Daisies. Uranne, the
Pride of him who now, alas! was no more. Perchance
He too was sleeping in that far-off land,
Without a kindly hand to smooth his aching
Brow, or wipe from his cheeks the damp
Death dews.

One morning when the dew
Had not yet left the sodden grass,
She left the cot to look for her beloved.
She sat her down 'mid the dingy rocks, which
Girt the shore. The little ripples kissed her feet
Caressingly. Long she looked for a white sail,
To greet her tired eyes.

Marco, dost hear Uranne's
Call? Wilt thou no more return? My heart is
Breaking with its load. No longer can I wait,—
But list! I'll whisper in thine ear,—
The blue "Forget-Me Nots,
The sweet Forget Me Nots" which thou
Did'st place upon my breast. Thou wilt see them
When thou com'st. None shall them remove.
Sweetheart, I keep them till you come.

There they found her cold
And stark. With hand pressed close to heart
Where lay her flowers. The sounding sea seemed
To forget to hurl its billows 'gainst the beach
Now white and shining. E'en the little ripples
Seemed to say, Uranne! And the great
Mountain rocks would echo back, Uranne!

Years went by. The war, the
Cruel war was at an end. And Peace with
Flowing mantle had overspread the land;—
With anxious heart, but willing feet, the

Soldier started for his dear old cabin nestled
So snugly in the valley. Would he find them all?

The dear old sire with his silvered hair—Perchance
He had lain him down to sleep, beside the wife
Who had left him in his prime.

But she, the dear
Uranne, she was there, no doubt of that. A stronger,
Healthier lass ne'er spun the dance.
Then the baby, our baby. How she must have
Grown. Wonder if she remembers me, her own dear
Sire? Who oft would soothe and rock to sleep.
O yes; Uranne has taught her to love and lisp
My name.

When the proud vessel dropped her
Anchor in the Bay, no prouder man, nor
Hopeful, than was Marco. Lightly he sprang
Ashore. He looked to right, to left, no sign of
His loved ones cheered his gaze.
Uranne, he cried, What! no welcome for Marco?
No outstretched arms to fold me in love's embrace?
He tottered to the cot all overgrown with
Weeds and trailing vines. O! stars above write
On hardest stone, Desolate, forlorn—alone.

Unconsciously he moved along the lane
That led to the old church-yard. The little
Tuneful bell that had pealed so joyously
On his marriage eve, was silent now.
He saw no one, nor questions asked. But
Slowly crept to where three mounds were
Raised all side by side. He closely scanned
Them all, when lo! upon the longest grave,
A beauteous tuft of blue Forget-Me-Nots—
Aha! he cried, my bright, my blue Forget-Me-Nots!

My flowers which I placed upon her breast,
And bid her wear till we should meet again,
My faithful one. The seeds matured on thy
Dear bosom, nourished by thine own mortality,
Pushed their way to the sunlight of earth, To
Cheer and to 'mind of faithful love,
Love which lasts even after the gates of
Death are passed. Then tie wailed the whole
Day long: Come, O! come! Uranne, come!
Like my flowers, leave your bed, too dark too
Drear for thee. Uranne, come to me!
Or I will come to thee!

There they found him, there they laid him,
With his flowers and Uranne.

Magnolia

Magnolia! "Pale city of the dead,"
Adown thy gravelled walks I tread,
Thy marble pillars looming high,
Thy polished shafts around me lie.
With soft, mild rays, the winter sun
Thy tortuous pathways doth illume,
The weeping-willow droops its head,
To crown the "City of the Dead."

On every side death's tracks I see,
His footsteps grim encompass me,
The high-born here, the lowly there,
The proud man there, the humble here.
The rich has left his golden hoard,
No more he sits at festive board,
He could not bribe relentless death,
With all his garnered stores of wealth.

Here lies a maiden spotless fair,
Whose claim on life for many a year
Seemed sure. But the grim Reaper smiled,
And bending, claimed her for his child.
So lovingly they made her bed.
And tenderly these garlands spread,
Bright emblems of a stricken flower,
Now blooming in a sunnier bower.

And here an infant's grave I see,
Ere sin could stain its purity,
It plumed its wings and upward soared,
To live forever with its God.
Though fair the earth, it would not stay,
Much fairer still the land away,
Restrain me not, for I would go
Where crystal fountains endless flow.

With slow, sad steps I press me on
To a majestic tower of stone,
That tells me they who sleep around
Had for their country's weal laid down
Their lives. Ah! many a widowed heart
Hath bent and broke with sorrow's dart,
For him who now beneath the sod,
Yielded his spirit to his God.

And many a youth with trappings gay,
'Mid martial music liveliest, lay,
No more in life returned to bless
Their loved ones with a fond caress,
But laid them down to their last sleep
In stranger land. Now angels keep
A loving vigil o'er each grave,
And bending branches o'er them wave.

City of Shadows! fondly keep
The loved who in thy bosom sleep,
Shielded from every earthly care,
They rest secure and free from fear.
Let grasses green and flow'rets bright,
Always illume thy paths with light,
Till from the heavens loud and clear,
Resounds the invitation dear,
"Come up and meet me in the air,
My people."

To My Mother

I took up the burden of life anew
When she, the pure-hearted, died;
When the golden cord was rent in twain,
And she faded from my side.
When the eyes grew dim that were wont to glow
With the holy light of love,
And the spirit, freed from earthly care,
Sped to its rest above.

Oh, the dreary days! Oh, the weary nights!
Oh, the anguish, who can tell?
When the light of my life went swiftly out,
And the shadow athwart me fell.
For the wound was deep, and the woe was great,
And its poignancy will blight
All the onward course of my future years,
Till my faith be turned to sight.

I muse me now of the beautiful days,
The halcyon days of yore;
And wonder if e'er on life's stormy sea
Such days I shall ever see more.
The sky is as blue-tinted now as then,
And the sunlight just as bright;
But they gladden me not as in other days
Ere she faded from my sight.

The clouds with their purple and amber hues—
Their gossamer robes of snow—
And the stars at the quiet twilight hour
In calm, clear beauty glow.
And music sweet as Æolian harp
Is echoing far and wide—
But, sure, naught gladdens my heart as before
She faded away from my side.

O, Mother! in anguish I peer through the mists
Of a future, so dark without thee;
The desert of life hath truly been blessed
With an oasis sacred to thee.
And oft to this green spot of beauty I turn,
My shrine of affection, my pride;
For, surely, naught gladdens my heart as before
Thou fadedst away from my side.

Nestle-Down Cottage

As I sit by the ruddy oak fire,
And feel the grateful glow,
Come mem'ries sweet of a rustic cot,
That stood near the pebbly shore.

With its porch so bright and sunny,
Where the children loved to play,
With the sounding shells, from the sandy beach,
All through the summer's day.

Where, where are the blessed little ones
Whose childish voices sweet,
Who made the sunny porch resound
With the patter of little feet?

One where the South Seas wildly break,
And dash on the gleaming sand,
Has made him a home 'mid strangers,
Far, far from his native land.

Another, the sweetest and dearest,
Has long 'neath the daisies been laid,
O! dark as a pall was the hour
When they whispered my darling was dead.

The cottage still stands by the sea shore,
Our sunny, bright *"Nestle-Down,"*
But we ask so sadly where, O! where
Are the little children gone?

Mother's Recall

Come back to me, O ye, my children;
Come back to the home as of yore;
As my longing eye peers through the vista of years,
Comes the heart-throbbing more and more.
I sit by the casement and listen
To the fall of the soft, sobbing rain,
E'en the winds gently sigh as if loth to reply—
In vain, fond mother, in vain.

Are ye gone for aye? Shall I no more hear
The ring and the din of glee?
Have my nestlings flown and left me alone?
Shall their faces, I no more see?
I sit, and I wait while the days go by,
And the months merge slow into years;
Till the twilight deep and the mystic sleep,
And the hopes give place to fears.

When the Christmas chimes with its holy rhymes
Ring out o'er the frosty plain,
Then I sit, and sigh for the "Sweet bye and bye"—
But the answer comes, "Mother in vain."
Each one of us, children, have gone forth
To fight out life's battles alone;
And the future must prove if your labor of love,
Has, like bread on the waters, been thrown.

So the twilight comes—and the fire burns low—
And the day is ebbing fast—
Soon the merry chimes and the hallowed rhymes
Will be numbered with the Past.
But with hopeful eyes I'll scan the skies,
Perchance, ere next Christmas-tide,
Will my children come to their own dear home.
And their place at mother's side.

Dedicated to the Right Rev'd D. A. Payne

Oh! surely 'tis a theme sublime
That stirs my soul today;
Awake then, muse nor slumber more,
Till sung the wondrous lay.
My song shall be of one, whose youth
And strength were freely given
To elevate, instruct, and lead
Benighted souls to heaven.

My song shall be of him, whose hand
A mother's taste did mould;
Whose precepts noble were to her
As apples of pure gold.
I'll tell of one whose virtues rare
In modesty enshrined;
Who bears a lasting laurel wreath
About his brow entwined.

Who in the days that tried men's souls
Did ne'er from duty quail,
But wrought on ensign, lifted high,
There's no such word as fail!
Mem'ries so sweet are hov'ring round,
That I, with Psalmist, say
"O! had I wings like turtle dove,
Quickly I'd fly away!"

Away, away beyond the hills
Where blooms the tree of life,
Where limpid streams whose silent flow,
Ne'er stir the sea of strife.
Oh! Bishop, Pastor, Friend, may'st thou
To green old age be spared;
Then, like a fully ripened ear
Go to thy rich reward.

October

Bright and beautiful art thou,
Autumn flowers crown thy brow,
Golden-rod and Aster blue,
Russet leaf with crimson hue.
Half stripped branches waving by,
Softly as a lullaby,
Tell of summer's days gone by,
Tell that winter's very nigh.

In the forest cool and chill,
Sadly moans the Whippoorwill,
Not as in the summer days,
When he gloried in his lays,
Lower-toned, but sweet and clear,
Like thy crisp and fragrant air,
Warbling forth with voice sublime,
This is nature's harvest time.

Crickets chirp amid the leaves,
Squirrels hop among the trees,
Brown nuts falling thick and fast,
On the dewy, dying grass,
Glowing sun with softer rays,
Harbinger of wintry days,
Tell the year is going by,
Sighing forth its lullaby.

The Dying Girl

Sister darling, ope the window, let the balmy air once more
Fan my flushed and throbbing brow as in the happy days of yore;
I would gaze again in rapture on the brightly setting sun
For I know, my gentle sister, that the goal is almost won.

See the crimson clouds are hov'ring round the glorious orb of day,
And the far-off hills are basking in its golden, garnished ray;
Listen to yon forest warbler hymning sweet and joyous lay,
Chanting forth its evening vespers to the sinking god of day.

But sister, time is waning, after all it doth but seem
That life is but a toilsome march, a weariness, a dream;
And yet I do not murmur, for if all the joys of earth
Had not faded from my vision ere they ripened into birth,

If the shadows had not thickened as they clustered round my brow,
Had I not turned from the altar, where I worshipped long ago,
Perchance I might have reveled full too deep in human love,
And forgotten God, my Maker, and my happy home above.

So 'tis well, and now I'm going to join that spirit band,
With their never-ceasing music, making glad that starry land;
And I'm glad too, for I'm weary, and would rest me from my woe—
Fain would land my stricken spirit on the banks of "Evermore."

And O! my dearly loved one, when sorrows round thee press,
Hurling each deadly missile on thy pure and youthful breast—
Then think upon thy dear one, O! may ne'er thy foot steps rove!
But meet me, surely meet me, in that happy home above.

Alaska

With thy rugged, ice-girt shore,
Draped in everlasting snow,
Thou'rt enthroned a queen.
Crown of moss and lichen grey,
Frosted o'er with ocean spray.
All thy long, long wintry day,
Dark and stern thy mien.

From the cloudland fresh and fair,
Falls the snow through crispy air,
Mantling vale and hill.
Then old "Borealis" glows,
With his fiery light that shows,
Frozen nature in repose,
River, stream and rill.

Oh thy north the Polar Sea
Thunders forth in wild meleè,
'Mid gorges dark and steep
Full many a ship with noble crew,
Lies low beneath thy waters blue,
Nor left behind a single clew,
But sleep a dreamless sleep.

Beside the far famed Yukon stands
Hundreds of men from distant lands,
All with the same desire.
Gold, gold's the watchword, yellow ore,
That tempts him from his homestead door,
And Oh! alas he nevermore
May sit by household fire.

Ah! if men would only toil,
Dig and delve their own rich soil,
With vigor and with vim;
Forth would spring the golden corn,

Loud would ring the harvest song,
Life and health they would prolong,
All through nature's prime.

Under his own, his fruitful vine,
Beneath his laden fig tree green,
He, like a king, would reign.
Bending low with purple yield,
Rivalling fair Eschkol's fields,
He'd a potent influence wield,
With his corn and wine.

On Parting with a Friend

Can I forget thee? No, while mem'ry lasts,
Thine image like a talisman entwined,
Around my heart by sacred friendship's ties
Remains unchanged, in love, pure love, enshrined.

Can I forget thee? Childhood's happy hours
Would like some flitting phantom mock and jeer;
Life's sunny hours, would quickly lose their charm,
If Lethe's slumbrous waves but touched me there.

Can I forget thee? 'Tis a sad, sad thought,
That friend from friend should thus be ruthless riven—
But list, methinks, a sweet voice whispers low,
Remember, no adieus are spoke in heaven.

Can I forget thee? No, though ocean's waves
May madly leap and foam 'twixt you and me,
Still o'er my stricken heart this yearning will remain,
Nor time estrange my love, dear one, from thee.

And though on earth again we never more may meet,
In that bright Elysian where spirits, holy, dwell,
May we in concert with that transported throng,
Unite, ne'er more (rapt thought) to say "farewell!"

Twilight Musings

I'm sitting by the hearthstone now,
And my heart is lone and drear;
It seems as though the autumn blast
Had left its impress there.
As memory, backward, wends its way,
Unfolding to my gaze
Those joyful hours of "Auld Lang Syne,"
Those lights of by-gone days.

I'm musing on the past, when I
In childhood's thoughtless play,
Reveled in gladness, joy and mirth,
Nor deemed one saddening ray
Should ever cloud my gladsome heart,
Or cause deep sorrow's moan—
Ne'er dreaming of the time, alas!
When I'd be quite alone.

I've listened to the morning's song
Of nature's feathered gems,
Long ere Aurora's roseate hue
Illumined Orient's realms,
And as their carols wafted high
On balmy zephyrs borne,
'Tis then I muse, and sadly feel,
That I am quite alone.

I've never heard the ocean's roar,
Or felt its quivering thrill;
Nor, on stern Neptune's bosom been,
When all was calm and still—
But o'er my heart, at times, there are
Such stormy billows borne,
That then I sadly, truly feel,
That I am quite alone.

Song to Erin

Oh! Erin my country, my ancestor's home!
Impelled by my wants, I, from thee, had to roam;
And now my heart yearneth, sore longeth for thee
My dear native Ireland, my "gem of the sea."

Oh! Erin my country, thou land of the brave!
Who'll rescue from tyr'ny, who'll ransom and save?
Thy despots so strong, are still wielding their power,
To bind thee in slavery both now and forever.

Speak! speak! who will rescue our Emerald Isle?
Now bowed by the oppressor in servitude vile!
Her sons are all scattered, her daughters are gone,
And she is left desolate, forlorn and alone.

I'll sigh for thee Erin, when spring winds doth fan,
With musical breathings, this far distant land;
'Twill remind me of youth's happy days on thy shore—
Of days, mournful thought, I shall never see more.

I'll weep for thee Erin, as the blue waters surge,
Shall re-echo my wailing, shall chant the sad dirge;
Of Ireland in slavery, once land of the free;
Of Ireland, my country, my "gem of the sea."

The Valentine

Lady with thine eyes of beauty
Rivaling cerulean flowers,
Where the love-beams seem to linger,
Throughout youth's bright, sunny hours.

With thy smile of witching sweetness
Like the magnet's mystic art,
Charming oft enchanting oft'ner,
Drawing to thee every heart.

But, fair lady, I'll no longer
Linger thus o'er nature's mould,
'Tis thy spirit's beauty charms me,
More than mines of Peru's gold.

Like an exile who hath wandered
Far from kindred and from home,
Pants and longs once more to greet them,
Never more on earth to roam;—

Like the tempest-tossed, the weary,
Who of earth ne'er had their part,
Fain would land their stricken spirits
Where heart answers unto heart;—

So this bosom when o'erflowing
With some latent, deadly grief,
Loves to revel in the music
Of thy voice to find relief.

And when joys do hover 'round me,
Weaving chaplets rich and bright,
I'd away from pleasures turn me
To my beautiful "Starlight."

Lady! could I seal thy future,
All of bliss and love 'twould be;
And when time with us is ended,
Spend eternity with thee.

LINES TO FLORENCE

I am sitting sad and lonely
Where I've often sat before,
And I am musing, fondly musing
Of my Florence who pass'd o'er.
Pass'd into the realms supernal,
Far 'bove cloud-lands lofty height;
Yonder 'mid the fields Elysian,
Dwells my "Flor" 'mong saints of light.

'Twas when autumn leaves were falling,
'Twas when harvest days had come,
That, King Death, the mighty reaper,
Came to take my darling home.
When the winds were softly sighing,
Zephyrs breathing low and deep,
Lulled to rest by such sweet music,
My bright treasure fell asleep.

Closely clasped to mother's bosom
On the well-nigh bursting breast,
Lay the early stricken floweret,
Lay the heart so near its rest.
And those little eyes upturning,
Brimful with their wealth of love,
Mutely, though with earnest language,
Said, I'm hastening up above.

Well, ere long, they said my darling
Had this earth exchanged for heaven—
She had upward spread her pinions,
Leaving hearts with anguish riven.
Yes; the autumn's wind so plaintive,
With its music soft and deep,
Woo'd my birdie from my bosom,
And she sweetly fell asleep.

But when time with me is over,
When my fleeting years have passed,
Oh! I trust once more to greet her,
And this parting be the last;
So till then I wait expectant—
I, the Master's time doth "bide"—
But to me the hour is precious,
That my little Florence died.

"By the Rivers of Babylon"

By the Rivers of Babylon we mournfully bent,
With "harps on the willows" and vesture all rent,
For burdened by sorrow and saddened by pain,
We felt that we no more could strike them again.

This, this is a strange land, we will not then sing
One song of our Zion, the home of our King,
No rather let right hand its cunning forget,
Than we to our loved home as recreants act.

O! City of God, though as captives we go
Jerusalem's weal we'll never forego,
O! soon may the exiles of Israel return,
To sing Zion's songs in their own holy land.

The Pen

Mightier than the sword thou art,
Thou can'st pierce like venomed dart,
Time and space count naught with thee,
Leagues of land or leagues of sea.

Thou can'st waves of passion calm,
Griefs assuage like Gilead's balm,
Bring sweet pleasure to the eye,
Give sweet gladness for the sigh.

When thy little point is prest,
Oft it wounds some gentle breast,
Filling chalice to the brim,
Darkening life with sorrows grim.

Learnéd sage in days gone by,
Scanned thee with prophetic eye,
Said to myriads then unborn
Thou would'st rule on many a throne.

Swords may stab with savage ire
Glistening out like rays of fire,
They can ne'er thy power attain,
O'er the sea or o'er the main.

Mightier than the sword art thou,
Lo! on many a regal brow
Furrows which thy point has wrought,
Troubles which thy work has brought.

Mightier than the sword art thou,
List! a maid records her vow,
That so long as life shall last,
Ne'er a doubt shall love o'ercast

Naught of bliss or naught of woe,
But thou can'st on man bestow,
With thy tiny pointed prow,
Mightier than the sword art thou.

Passing of the Old Year

Ah! the year is slowly dying,
And the wind in tree-top sighing,
Chant his requiem.
Thick and fast the leaves are falling,
High in air wild birds are calling,
Nature's solemn hymn.

In the deep, dark forest lingers,
Imprints of his icy fingers,
Chill, and dark, and cold.
And the little streamlets flowing,
Wintry sun so softly glowing,
Through the maple's gold.

So, Old Year, gird on your armor,
Let not age, nor fear, nor favor,
Hurry you along.
List! the farewell echoes pealing,
List! the midnight hour is stealing,
Hark! thy dying song.

Say, Old Year, ere yet your death knell
Rings from out yon distant church bell,
Say, what have you done?
Tell of hearts you've sadly broken,
Tell of love dead and unspoken,
Ere your course is run.

Tell the mother who doth languish,
O'er her graves in silent anguish,
She will see again,
Blooming bright "beyond the river,"
Living on for aye and ever,
Every bright-eyed gem.

Ah! full many a spirit weary,
You have wooed from paths so dreary,
Wafted them above.
Now they say *Old Year,* we bless thee,
Raise thy head, we would caress thee
For this home of love.

On thy brow lies many a furrow,
And thy eyes tell many a sorrow
Hath its shadow cast.
But thy task is almost ended,
Soon the path which thou hast wended,
Will be called the *"Past."*

Then, old dying year we hold thee,
To our hearts we fondly fold thee,
Ere the midnight bell.
Soon thy race will now be ended,
With Eternity be blended,
So, Old Year, farewell.

Sonnet to My First Born

Oh! waves in the sunlight gleaming,
Oh! billows with ceaseless roar,
Bring back to this aching heart of mine,
The laddie you bore long ago.
Far out on on your restless bosom,
Far away from his boy-hood's home,
I charge you waves of the deep, blue sea
To bid my wanderer come.

Oh! stars in the heavens twinkling
Like lamps hung up in the sky,
Oh! moon look down through the darkness,
His trysting-place you may descry.
Then tell him a fond heart is aching,
In love for the dear one she bore,
Oh! surely to thee he will hearken,
And haste to his own cottage door.

The winds of the autumn are sighing,
The leaves from the trees falling fast,
The roses that erstwhile were blooming,
Say mournfully—Summer is past.
The daisies have long ago slumbered,
Their blossoms I search for in vain;
But surely for thee I will look, love,
Ere spring time brings them again.

When the Frost-King's robe is glistening
O'er hill, and valley, and glen,
When the bright sleigh-bells are jingling,
I know he'll come to me then.
So sunlight, or starlight, or moonlight,
Wherever my truant you see,
Just tell him you left me a-waiting
Far over the deep blue sea.

LINES TO—

O come to me in my dreams love!
When the world is wrapped in sleep,
And the silver moon like virgin queen,
Her lonely vigils keep.
When all is hushed in calm repose—
The earth, and sky, and sea,
Then hasten love to this far-off land,
And dwell one hour with me.

O come to me in my dreams love!
And cheer me on my way;
And bid me look to a higher land
For the dawn of a brighter day.
Then breathe to heaven an earnest prayer
To bless, ere you depart,
With perfect love and childlike faith,
This sad, despondent heart.

O, do not forget to come, love,
But on rosy pinions haste,
And deluge my willing ear, with
Momentoes of the past.
And tell me, too, of that distant land,
Its sunshine and its flowers;
And in return my strain shall be
Magnolia's bright bowers.

Ah, do not fail to come love,
For I'll woo my slumber tonight;
I'll lay me down to sweet repose,
And wait for thee and light.
Then hie to my bower on wings of love,
Ah, linger not by the way,
But solace this heart and bid it hope,
For the dawn of a brighter day.

Highland Mary

Will you leave the hills of Scotland?
Your childhood's happy home,
To brave the dangers of the deep,
In foreign lands to roam—
Say, Mary, will you, for my sake
Leave yonder joyous cot—
Your youthful friends and scenes so dear,
To share a soldier's lot?

The battle's din, my Mary,
Has never met thine ear,
The woodlands' songsters melody
Is all that thou dost hear.
The vivid flash of musketry—
The cannon's thundering roar
Must meet thine eye, burst on thine ear
Sounds never heard before.

And now, fond one, I've told you all,
And I can say no more—
"Will you go to the Indies, my Mary,
And leave old Scotia's shore?"

The Cherokee

'Twas a cloudless morn and the sun shone bright,
And dewdrops sparkled clear;
And the hills and the vales of this Western land
Were wreathed with garlands rare.
For verdant spring with her emerald robe
Had decked the forest trees;
Whilst e'er and anon the vine-clad boughs
Waved in the playful breeze.

All, all was still, not a sound was heard,
Save the music of each tree,
As gracefully it bent and bowed
Its branches o'er the lea.
But hark! a sound, 'tis the Red man's tread,
Breaks on the silent air;
And a sturdy warrior issues forth,
Robed in his native gear.

And wandering on, he neared the brook;
Then sat him down to rest;
'Twas a noble sight—that warrior free—
That Monarch of the West.
He gazed around, O! a wistful gaze
Saddened his upturned brow,
As he thought of those he'd fondly loved,
Of those now laid so low.

He mused aloud "Great Spirit!" list
To the Indian's earnest plea;
And tell me why, from his own loved home,
Must the Indian driven be.
When the "Pale Face" came to our genial clime,
We wondered and were glad;
Then hied us to our chieftain's lodge,
Our noble "Flying Cloud."

We told him all, and he calmly said
He'd gladly give them place;
And if friends they proved, perchance, extend
The calumet of peace.
But soon, alas! the dread truth rang
That the Pale Face was our foe;
For he made our warriors bite the dust—
Our children lie so low.

So now, my own, dear, sunny land,
Each woodland and each dell,
Once the Indian's home, now the Indian's grave,
I bid a last farewell.
To the "Great Spirit's" hunting-ground,
To meet my long-lost bride,
My "Raven Wing" I gladly hie—
He said, then calmly died.

Rally Song

Come, let us join this festal lay—
Hurra, Hurra,
Come, let us join this festal lay,
And let our anthems all be gay,
And sing aloud for this glad day
Should brighten every heart:—

We'll sing of heroes who have fought—
Hurra, Hurra,
We'll sing of heroes who have fought,
Who to their country's altar brought,
And on her sacred ensign wrought,
The tree of liberty

We'll sing of martyrs who have died—
Hurra, Hurra,
We'll sing of martyrs who have died,
From severed ranks, as side by side
They bravely stemmed the gory tide,
To ransom brother man.

Our glorious banner's now unfurled—
Hurra, Hurra,
Our glorious banner's now unfurled,
May it soon wave o'er all the world,
And every traitor standard hurled
From pinnacle to earth.

With gifted leaders in our van—
Hurra, Hurra,
With gifted leaders in our van,
The bright and noblest of our land,
Let patriots shout, as, hand in hand,
They welcome this glad day.

SERENADE

Sleep, love sleep,
The night winds sigh,
In soft lullaby.
The Lark is at rest
With the dew on her breast.
So close those dear eyes,
That borrowed their hue
From the heavens so blue,
Sleep, love sleep.

Sleep, love sleep,
The pale moon looks down
On the valleys around,
The Glow Moth is flying,
The South wind is sighing,
And I am low lying,
With lute deftly strung,
To pour out my song,
Sleep, love sleep

The Coming Woman

Just look, 'tis a quarter past six, love—
And not even the fires are caught;
Well, you know I must be at the office—
But, as usual, the breakfast 'll be late.

Now hurry and wake up the children;
And dress them as fast as you can;
"Poor dearies," I know they'll be tardy,
Dear me, "what a slow, poky man!"

Have the tenderloin broiled nice and juicy—
Have the toast browned and buttered all right;
And be sure you settle the coffee:
Be sure that the silver is bright.

When ready, just run up and call me—
At eight, to the office I go,
Lest poverty, grim, should o'ertake us—
"'Tis bread and butter," you know.

The bottom from stocks may fall out,
My bonds may get below par;
Then surely, I seldom could spare you
A nickel, to buy a cigar.

All ready? Now, while I am eating,
Just bring up my wheel to the door;
Then wash up the dishes; and, mind now,
Have dinner promptly at four;

For tonight is our Woman's Convention,
And I am to speak first, you know—
The men veto us in private,
But in public they shout, "That's so."

So "by-by"—In case of a rap, love,
Before opening the door, you must look;
O! how could a civilized woman
Exist, without a man cook.

ODE TO PEACE

Come Peace, on snowy pinions,
Come, nestle like a dove;
Encircle earth's dominions
With harmony and love.
Let anger, pride and malice,
And strife forgotten lie;
Nor from their venomed chalice,
Quaff more bitter draughts and die.

Come Peace, with arms extended,
Come, brood o'er this fair land;
Let battle scenes be ended,
And heart be joined with hand.
Let fields now crimsoned over,
With the life-blood of the brave,
Loom as monuments of warning,
Shine, as beacon lights to save.

Come Peace, a welcome waits thee,
From many a stricken life;
And many a heart-crushed mourner,
Now weary of the strife;
Methinks e'en now a footfall
Breaks like music on my ear,
As the distant sound of gladness,
When 'tis borne on summer's air.

May the echoes prove prophetic;
May thy murmurs from afar
Shed a radiance as refulgent,
Beam as bright as Bethlehem's Star.
And the hearts that have been riven,
And the bosoms that have bled,
Soon will change their griefs to gladness,
Yield to God and earth their dead.

A Reverie

You may speak of a grave in a distant land,
Or of one 'neath ocean's foam,
Where the dolphins play o'er the sunny spray,
Far from the dear old home;
Where the coral peaks form a glorious tomb,
And the mighty waters lave,
But there is naught in the wide world sought
Like the heart's deep anguished grave.

You may tell of a grave 'neath the burning sands
Of the tropics fevered zone;
Where silence reigns o'er the desert plains
So desolate, so forlorn.
Where the lion's roar is the liveliest sound
That o'er that waste is heard—
And the forest bird hymns a plaintive lay,
A requiem for the dead.

Again you may tell of a grave unsought
Far from the home of youth;
Where the willow weeps as the exile sleeps
Akin to Mother Earth.
But O! methinks, there's not a woe
That can the bosom cleave,
Or as deeply wound, as the lowly mound
O'er the heart's deep, anguished grave.

SUNSET

All hail! thou gorgeous sunset,
With thy gold and purple clouds,
Tinting the vast horizon,
Like shadowy, fleecy shrouds.

The mountain crests are glowing,
The hills are crimson dyed,
The very air seems blushing,
Bathed in thy amber tide.

Soon the twilight shadows falling
Will thy glory chase away,
And weary man will welcome
The closing of the day.

Then the moon in silvery brightness,
Will show her pale, sad face;
And the stars as her attendants,
Will stud infinite space.

Low down amid the valley
Soon we'll hear the night-bird's song,
Calling softly to the south wind,
That the day of toil is done.

Then hail! thou glorious sunset,
Who in fullness can portray
The varied, wondrous beauty
Of a summer's sunset day.

THE PAST

The Past it is fraught with many a feeling
Of pleasure, of sadness, of joy, and of pain;
And 'tis sweet of an eve when dewdrops are falling,
To reflect on the days that can ne'er come again.

The Past, it is pleasant! Ah, memory recalls
The period of childhood, when joyous and free,
With innocence crowned, in purity robed,
We revelled in gladness and sported in glee.

The Past, it is saddening! full many a loved one
That joined in each pleasure, partook of each pain,
Have passed on before, to the spirit land flown,
And left us below, till their prize we attain.

The Past's irrevocable! every word we've spoken,
Or action committed, been stamp'd with its seal
Immortal, enduring, 'twill stand sure forever,
As no time can efface, nor effulgence reveal.

Then, then, should the Present be valued and used
As a boon from the Author and Giver of gifts;
That so, when 'tis past, we could always enjoy
The pleasant assurance of its being well spent.

Marriage

The die is cast, come weal, come woe,
Two lives are joined together,
For better or for worse, the link
Which naught but death can sever.
The die is cast, come grief, come joy,
Come richer, or come poorer,
If love but binds the mystic tie,
Blest is the bridal hour.

For Who?

When the heavens with stars are gleaming
Like a diadem of light,
And the moon's pale rays are streaming,
Decking earth with radiance bright;
When the autumn's winds are sighing,
O'er the hill and o'er the lea,
When the summer time is dying,
Wanderer, wilt thou think of me?

When thy life is crowned with gladness.
And thy home with love is blest,
Not one brow o'ercast with sadness,
Not one bosom of unrest—
When at eventide reclining,
At thy hearthstone gay and free,
Think of one whose life is pining,
Breathe thou, love, a prayer for me.

Should dark sorrows make thee languish,
Cause thy cheek to lose its hue,
In the hour of deepest anguish,
Darling, then I'll grieve with you.
Though the night be dark and dreary,
And it seemeth long to thee,
I would whisper, "be not weary;"
I would pray love, then, for thee.

Well I know that in the future,
I may cherish naught of earth;
Well I know that love needs nurture,
And it is of heavenly birth.
But though ocean waves may sever
I from thee, and thee from me,
Still this constant heart will never,
Never cease to think of thee.

June

I am the month when roses
Bloom brightest o'er the glade,
I am the month when marriages
Most happily are made.

Mine is the time of foliage,
When hills and valleys teem
With buds and vines sweet scented,
All clothed in glowing green.

My nights are bright and starry,
My days are long and clear
And truly I'm the fairest,
Of all months in the year.

With night dews gently falling,
With bees upon the wing,
And tiny rills soft rippling
Amid the valleys sing.

The farmer with his ploughshare,
Swift turning up the sod,
His brawny arms at labor,
His soul with Nature's God.

The Lark with sweetest carol,
Doth greet the rising sun,
The Mock-bird at the even,
Loud whistles day is done.

O! I'm the month of beauty,
The summer's crown I claim,
Now whisper to me softly,
And tell me what's my name.

Tribute to a Lost Steamer

O! sing ye a dirge for the loved and the lost,
That have found them a home 'neath the coral reefs deep;
That have laid them to rest 'neath the murmuring surge,
Where the whistling wind wails o'er their sweet, but sad sleep.

They have gone to their home—their last resting-place
The blue waves embraced and called them their own;
While the depths of the sea and the billows thereof
Are mournfully sighing their sad requiem.

Down, down through the mass of the waters they sped,
Amid the dark chambers so mystic, so drear;
'Till perchance they selected some ruby-lit bed,
To sleep their last sleep 'mid jeweled gems rare.

O! 'tis sweet now to ponder, though many have gone
To that far-off bourne whence no traveller returns,
That the sea shall not always their bodies retain,
For Jehovah hath said, she must yield them again.

One bright little jewel outlived the dark storm,
So fatal to many, yet—blissful to tell—
His "Father in heaven" preserved him from harm,
O, parent rejoice! with your *Louis* 'tis well.

A Requiem

O, insatiable monster! Could'st thou not
In pity turn aside thy venomed shaft
From her my gifted, darling friend?
Has sympathy within thy breast
No trysting place? That thou must come
At spring-time when the flowerets bloom
To bear my loved one to the tomb?

So young was she; life's woes had not yet dimmed
The joyous sunshine of her girlhood's days;
She did not quaff the dregs of time,
But, like some rosebud prematurely culled,
She sped away, and o'er her grave
So peacefully the willows wave
And dewdrops, her calm bosom lave.

Tread not the earth where sleeps my loved one's form;
But place it lightly on her marble brow.
Bid birdies sing at set of sun
To gladden Fannie's lowly home;
Bid rippling springs with shining spray,
And sylvan notes and songsters lay
Unite, to chase the gloom away.

Blest child! she did not tarry long, and yet,—
O, happy thought—she did not live in vain,
If truly she did seek and find
The "Pearl of Price," that precious boon,
Then ne'er to her could come too soon
The summons to an early tomb.

Blest child, rest! while gentle zephyrs breathe
Their fragrance through the waving trees;
All nature decked in gorgeous array

Is reveling now, but soon alas!
Like thee, 'twill fade. The autumn's knell
Will ere long peal like funeral bell.
Its dirge like sounds, "Friend, fare thee well."

THE GRAFTED BUD

Life's stormy surge had scarcely touched
Her blooming, beauteous brow,
When rudely torn from earthly bliss,
A budded, broken flower.

Methinks I see her brilliant eye,
When smiles played softly there,
As gentle as the summer's breeze,
So radiant, sweet and clear.

But ah! frail nature gave away,
And she was doomed to die,
So young in years, so bright, so fair,
In the cold grave to lie.

So to the realms of light and life
Her uncaged spirit fled;
There to remain until the trump
Shall sound to wake the dead.

There with the Saviour she abides,
There tunes the sacred lyre,
Regardless of th' impending day,
And dreading not its ire.

To a Loved One

I'll think of thee, mine own, dear one
As morn's first blushing ray
Diffuses light o'er the dim earth—
Turns darkness into day.

I'll think of thee at eve, my love,
When moon and star appear—
When in the horizon of my hope
All, all is bright and clear.

I'll think of thee when joy doth cast
Its gladness o'er my heart,
As peace, and love and happiness
Seem new life to impart.

I'll think of thee when dark shades fall
Athwart my fevered brow;
When low in death I hear thee lisp—
"I'm waiting for thee now."

I'll think of thee, my darling one,
While I have life and breath;
And seal the assurance fervently,
I'll think of thee in death.

The Nativity

The gloom of night had overspread the land,
Swaying its dread sceptre o'er every man;
For superstition like a monarch reigned,
And Adam's sons were fettered by its chain.

When the fulfilment of the promise came,
A Saviour! born today in Bethlehem;
Gabriel, the news, the joyful news revealed
By night, to some poor shepherds in the field.

Go now to Bethlehem, behold the Babe—
Though Lord of all, He's in a manger laid!
Among the horned cattle there you'll find
The Prince of Peace, the Saviour of mankind.

The Shepherds then in haste obeyed his word,
Guided by flaming star to view their Lord;
They entered in, when, judge of their surprise—
An infant, a Redeemer, burst upon their eyes.

Amazed, affrighted, trembling, they
Gazed on the Babe as there He lay;
Though in a manger yet He bore
Rare tokens of Almighty power.

To the Mock-Bird

Bird of the woodland, sing me a song,
Fain would I list to thee, all the day long.
Out from thy cosy nest, 'mid leafy bower,
Lift high thy tuneful voice—'tis summer's hour.

Bird of the forest, with voice sublime,
Gladdening with thy music all summer time,
E'en while the Autumn's winds bend low the trees,
Sweetly still thy carols float with the breeze.

Queen of the song-realm, what doest thou?
Up amid the leaflets, rocking on the bough,
Ah! little trickster, building thee a nest,
Cosy, soft and warm, for thy wee ones to rest.

Bird of the south-land, haste thee and bring
Tributes of thy melody, welcoming the spring,
Say to sombre winter—up and away,
This my time of minstrelsy, bright, sunny May

IN MEMORIAM

Rev. Samuel Weston

Oh! surely for thee were the gates ajar,
As thy chariot onward sped,
When with brightened eye and youth renewed,
Triumphant thou did'st tread
Through the gates of death, to the portals bright,
While the ransomed myriads sing,
"Lift up your heads, ye Golden Gates,"
Let the aged pilgrim in.

No terrors for thee had the darksome vale,
For like the wise virgins of old,
Thou keep'st thy lamp burning and trimmed from thy youth,
Till three-score and ten were well told.
And oft, as a shepherd, that tends his flock,
Thou did'st them to still waters lead,
And 'mid the green pastures of justified grace,
Thou lovedst thy children to feed.

Then Pastor and Leader, fond Parent, adieu,
Till the last, grand trump shall sound,
When shepherd and flock united once more,
Shall echo a long harvest home.

To Rev. Thaddeus Saltus

Sleep, Christian warrior, sleep,
Life's fitful dream is o'er,
Thy pain-tossed bark is anchored
Safe on the golden shore.
'Neath the green sward we lay thee
Thus early to thy rest,
And press the sod thus lightly,
Upon thy gentle breast.

Though but in manhood's prime,
When the dread summons came,
To hush the voice so well attuned
To preaching "In His Name."
Thou did'st not murmur, but with joy
Obeyed the Master's word,
And rapture crowned did'st enter
The palace of thy Lord.

Then sweetly sleep, dear Rector,
Thy grave we'll deck with flowers,
An earnest of that Better Land
Of ever blooming bowers.
Around this spot a halo twines,
While angels vigils keep,
And we rejoice that thus "He gives
To His beloved sleep."

Tribute to Capt. F. W. Dawson

Carolina mourns today. For he, the gifted
Son of her adoption, is no more. The voice
That stirred the bosoms of her sons, and
Made her ramparts ring from mount to
Sea-board, is hushed in death. His
Noble form, and nobler mien that
Never faltered 'mid the cannon's
Roar, lies motionless.

So Carolina weeps. 'Tis meet she should—
Her chieftain lieth low. In this
Grand, old City by the Sea, this Venice
Of the Southland. The home he loved
So well. When the grey morn breaks,
And when the twilight lingers, they
Chant in low, sweet music, evening
Vespers for his soul.

Then, Carolinians, build a monument for him;
But not on marble cold. Not on
Towering dome or polished shaft,
Should his memory be engraved. But
In the hearts of those he loved and
Served, should immortelles, perpetual, bloom;
And incense, fragrant, ever rise
To his memory.
Requiescat in Pace.

Mrs. Louise B. Weston

My Mother! With the angels now,
Life's race completely run;
The Pilgrim's cross is laid aside,
The Christian's crown is won.

Full two-score years has thy frail bark
Relentlessly been driven,
Along the rugged shoals of time—
Now safely moored in heaven.

Some vision bright of Eden's land—
Some glimpse from Nebo's crest—
So ravished thy enraptured soul,
Then panting for its rest,

That when the City bathed in gold
Full burst upon your sight,
You would not tarry with us more;
Your spirit took its flight.

My Mother, when life's sands run low,
In love, in kindness come,
And take the spirit of thy child,
And bid her "welcome home."

LINES TO MRS. ISABEL PEACE

'Tis said but a name is friendship,
 Soulless, and shallow, and vain;
That the human heart ne'er beats in response,
 Or echoes sweet sympathy's strain.

But today in "memory's mirror"
 Came a dear and honored one,
Whom in days gone by had lived and had loved,
 Ere her heavenly goal was won.

Her countenance beamed as of yore,
 With radiant smiles of love,
And I felt that the friendship she lavished me here,
 Had ripened in heaven above.

I felt that her voice so winsome,
 Attuned to holier rhymes,
Would in soft cadence tell of friendship's truth,
 Like harp of a thousand strings.

Rise up and call her blest!
 Ye children of her love,
For a friendlier hand or a kindlier heart
 Ne'er entered the mansions above.

Alphonse Campbell Fordham

Aged 6 Years, 2 Months, 20 Days

Almost whose last words were
"We shall meet beyond the River."
Yes, my darling, when life's shadows
Over me do darkly fall,
Meet me surely at the river
As I haste to obey the call.
Gladly through the darksome valley,
Through its portals, grim and cold,
Will I hasten 'till my nestling
Meets me at the "Gates of Gold."

Sadly do I miss my wee one,
None can fill thy vacant place,
Only in my dreams I fold thee,
Only then behold thy face.
See thee in thy childish beauty,
Clasp thy little hand in mine,
Ever will those moments chain me,
Ever in my heart enshrined.

Little Heartsease, "bud of promise,"
Broken off in early morn,
Now can sin no more pollute thee
In the angels' bosom borne.
In that land no pain or anguish
Ever can my child enfold,
Then my darling meet thy mother
Surely at the "Gates of Gold."

Mr. Edward Fordham

When the Autumn's breezes
Were sweeping o'er the land,
Came the mighty mandate
From the upper land.

Now from pain and anguish
Thou hast found relief,
Passed through death's dark portal,
Left this world of grief.

Now thou'rt safely anchored
In the port above,
Gladly do we offer thee
Symbols of our love.

When the welcome summons
Shall echo through the skies,
Then our ransomed brother
Will hear the word *"Arise."*

Death of a Grandparent

Mrs. Jennette Bonneau

Rest thee aged pilgrim, now thy toils are o'er;
Peacefully thou'st landed over Jordan's shore;
Safe from all the sorrows, free from all the strife,
Thou hast passed death's portals, entered into life.

Doubtless thou wert weary, tempest tossed so long;
Doubtless thou wert longing to join the happy throng;
Doubtless many loved ones on the other shore,
Whispered to thee softly " Stay on earth no more."

Whispered thee, come higher, where perennial bloom
Shall with heightened luster its wonted sway resume.
"Come where peaceful rivers quietly do flow—
Hasten mother, hasten, from that world of woe."

Then to fields Elysian she joyfully did soar,
In the blest land of Canaan to dwell forever more;
All through the "Golden City" she happily doth roam,
Oft wondering why she stay'd so long away from home.

So 'neath the bending willows we've laid thee down to rest,
Well knowing thou'rt reposing secure on Jesus' breast;
Well knowing that one day will come, the welcome word Arise,
Come up, thou ransomed mortal, to thy Saviour in the skies.

Queenie

For one brief day, did Queenie stay
To brighten each fond heart,
Then sped like dove to realms above,
Ne'er more to feel death's dart.

O! in that land, where infants stand
Arrayed in spotless sheen,
No griefs to share, nor sorrows bear,
No death to intervene.

We would not care, nay, would not dare
To wish thee back again,
Nay, rather say, "Queenie, good day,
Till we your rest attain."

To an Infant

Just as the twilight's holy hour
In quietude so deep,
Was hushing nature to repose,
Our "Charlie" fell asleep.

Just in the bloom of infancy,
We laid him to his rest,
Well knowing that our angel boy
Was numbered with the blest.

Well knowing that the Saviour said
Oh! suffer such to come,
"Forbid them not," for they are Mine,
And heaven is their home.

So bow we to God's gracious will,
For he was lent, not given,
And let this cheer our drooping hearts,
Our Charlie is in heaven.

Susan Eugenia Bennett

When the Sabbath was declining, just at twilight's mystic hour,
Left the " Upper Courts" an angel, sent to cull our sweetest flower,
Not in judgment, not in anger, did this white-winged seraph come,
But to lead a little Pilgrim through Death's Portal to her home.

And our angel child was ready, aye, and anxious to depart—
Not the slightest doubt o'ershadowed her trusting little heart;
But with a brow as radiant as rainbow in the sky,
She whispered softly "Mother, I'm not afraid to die. "

When shall these little, weary limbs lie down to sweet repose,
'Mid the green, the verdant pastures where the limpid water flows;
When shall I the Golden City sparkling in its beauty see,
"When shall it be, my Saviour, O! when shall I be free?"

Ere the week-day with its labors, its duties and its care—
Was ushered in, our darling was found on earth no where;
But with the saints in glory, and the Saviour she adored,
She's happy and at rest, for aye and ever with the Lord.

Mrs. Rebecca Weston

"For so He giveth His beloved sleep."
  She is not dead, but sleepeth;—
  Ere long will the morning break,
  When those we love who sleep in Him,
  Shall from the dust awake.

  She is not dead, but sleepeth;—
  Soon, soon will the ransomed sing
  O! grave, where is thy victory?
  O! death, where is thy sting?

Mrs. E. Cohrs Brown

Tread not the earth where lies her youthful form,
Grow violets, sweet violets, above that cherished mound;
Bid zephyrs softly whisper in accents sweet and low,
Not dead, not lost, but only gone a little while before.

So, I, though bowed in anguish, yield her spirit to its God,
And meekly clasp the smiting hand, and kiss the chast'ning rod;
May I, when time is over, greet thee on the other shore,
To live and love for aye and aye, where partings are no more.

Mrs. Mary Furman Weston Byrd

Obituary

Byrd.—"As one who wraps the drapery of his couch about him and lies down to pleasant dreams," thus sweetly passed from earth to glory, on the morning of the 19th of February, 1884, Mrs. Mary Furman Weston Byrd, in the 92d year of her age, leaving two children, twelve grand-children, and twenty great-grand-children, to mourn her irreparable loss.

"Rising up they call her blessed": Another ancient landmark has been gathered to her Fathers. With her death a link is severed which bound two centuries together. The venerable subject of this notice was born in 1792, of parents who were both exiles from their native land; one being born in Morocco, Barbary States, the other in Marseilles, France. During her eventful life she passed through three wars; that of 1812 in her girlhood, after the Mexican and the late Civil Wars. Possessed of a loving heart and cheerful disposition, charity was the guiding star of her life. Her widow's mite was never found wanting. In her the distressed and the needy met always a ready response. She died as she lived, beloved and venerated by legions to whom her very name was a household word. So then,

Though no blossoms cluster
Above thy aged brow,
Though winter winds are breathing
A requiem soft and low,
We look beyond earth's shadows,
Beyond death's misty plain,
And though we sadly miss thee,
Will not wish thee back again.

Could we but see time, dear one,
In the Palace of thy Lord,
With thy robe of snowy whiteness,
And with more than youth renewed.
No more on bended willows
Would our broken harps remain,
Take us beauty for our ashes,
Take us gladness for our pain.

A Note About the Author

Mary Weston Fordham (1862–1905) was an African American poet and educator. Born in Charleston, South Carolina, she was the daughter of Rev. Samuel Weston and Louise Bonneau. As a young woman, she worked for the American Missionary Association as a teacher. Towards the end of her life, Fordham published *Magnolia Leaves* (1897), a collection of sixty-six poems on African American life during the Reconstruction Era and beyond. While little is known about her life, it is suggested in her poetry that she suffered the loss of six children at a young age.

A Note from the Publisher

Spanning many genres, from non-fiction essays to literature classics to children's books and lyric poetry, Mint Edition books showcase the master works of our time in a modern new package. The text is freshly typeset, is clean and easy to read, and features a new note about the author in each volume. Many books also include exclusive new introductory material. Every book boasts a striking new cover, which makes it as appropriate for collecting as it is for gift giving. Mint Edition books are only printed when a reader orders them, so natural resources are not wasted. We're proud that our books are never manufactured in excess and exist only in the exact quantity they need to be read and enjoyed.

Discover more of your favorite classics with Bookfinity™.

- Track your reading with custom book lists.
- Get great book recommendations for your personalized Reader Type.
- Add reviews for your favorite books.
- AND MUCH MORE!

Visit **bookfinity.com** and take the fun Reader Type quiz to get started.

Enjoy our classic and modern companion pairings!